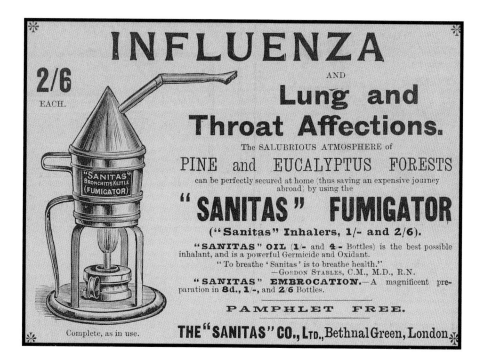

EPIDEMIC!

THE 1918 INFLUENZA PANDEMIC

by STEPHANIE TRUE PETERS

BENCHMARK BOOKS

MARSHALL CAVENDISH
NEW YORK

ACKNOWLEDGMENTS

The author wishes to thank Dr. Alfred W. Crosby, Professor Emeritus of the University of Texas at Austin and author of *America's Forgotten Pandemic*, Cambridge University Press, 1989, for his thoughtful reading of the manuscript.

Benchmark Books
Marshall Cavendish
99 White Plains Road
Tarrytown, New York 10591-9001
www.marshallcavendish.us

All Internet sites were available and accurate when this book was sent to press.

Book design by Michael Nelson

Library of Congress Cataloging-in-Publication Data

Peters, Stephanie True, 1965-
The 1918 influenza pandemic / by Stephanie True Peters.
p. cm. — (Epidemic!)
Summary: Describes the 1918 influenza pandemic, from how World War I soldiers spread the disease to recent scientific efforts to understand the virus that took between twenty and forty million lives worldwide.
Includes bibliographical references and index.
ISBN 0-7614-1636-6
1. Influenza—History—20th century—Juvenile literature. 2. Epidemics--History—20th century—Juvenile literature. [1. Influenza—History--20th century. 2. Epidemics—History—20th century. 3. Diseases.] I. Title II. Series: Peters, Stephanie True, 1965- . Epidemic!.

RC150.4.P48 2003
614.5'18'09041--dc22
2003022947

Picture Research by Linda Sykes Picture Research, Inc., Hilton Head, S. C.

Photo credits: Front cover: Hotel de Ville, Vichy, France/Giraudon/The Bridgeman Art Library International; 1: Illustrated London News, 1900/Mary Evans Picture Library; ii-iii: Galleria d'Arte Moderna, Florence, Italy/Alinari/ Bridgeman Art Library; vii, ix: Hulton/ Archive/Getty Images; x: Mary Evans Picture Library; 2, 3, 18, 21, 24, 27, 30, 33, 40: Brown Brothers; 4: Joe Readle/Getty Images; 7, 8: Getty Images; 10: Imperial War Museum, London/The Art Archive; 13: L'illustration War Album, September 25,1915, page 324/Mary Evans Picture Library; 14: AP Wide World Photos; 17,23, 29, back cover: National Library of Medicine, Washington, D. C.; 28, 35: Archive Photos/Getty Images; 36: Bettmann/Corbis; 37, 50: Hulton/Getty Images; 38: Imperial War Museum, London; 42: The Granger Collection; 46: Topical Press/Hulton Getty Images; 47: Illustrated London News, January 20, 1893, page 159/Mary Evans Picture Library; 48: Fox Photos/Hulton Getty Images; 52: University of Toronto Press; 55: Justin Sullivan/Getty Images; 58: Aventis Pasteur MSD/Getty Images

PRINTED IN CHINA

3 5 6 4

Front cover: 19th-century French painting of a father visiting his child in the hospital

Back cover: Influenza ward at Camp Funston, Kansas, around 1918

Half title: Early 20th-century British advertisement for an inhaler used to prevent influenza

Title page: 19th-century Italian painting of a hospital ward

From the Author, page vii: Photo of a baby, March 1939

CONTENTS

FROM THE AUTHOR

The idea for a series of books about epidemics came to me while I was sitting in the doctor's office with my son. He had had a sleepless, feverish night. I suspected he had an ear infection and looked forward to the doctor confirming my diagnosis and prescribing antibiotics.

While waiting for the doctor to appear, I suddenly realized that the situation I was in—a mother looking to relieve her child's pain—was hardly new. Humans have had an ongoing battle against disease throughout history. Today we have tremendous knowledge of how the human body works. We understand how viruses and bacteria attack and how the body defends itself. Through immunization and simple hygiene, we're often able to prevent disease in the first place. Our ancestors were not so knowledgeable, nor so lucky.

In this series, I have tried to put a human face on five epidemics that laid millions low. All five occurred in the past and have since been medically controlled. Yet in some areas of the world, similar stories are still being played out today as humans struggle against such enemies as AIDS, Ebola virus, hantavirus, and other highly contagious diseases. In the fight against disease, we may never have the upper hand. Microscopic foes are hard to fight.

THE FORGOTTEN PANDEMIC

There are several terms to describe the rapid and widespread occurrence of a disease. *Outbreak* is used when a disease suddenly infects many people within a small geographic area. *Epidemic* signifies that a great proportion of people in a certain geographic area have contracted the same disease within a short period of time. *Pandemic* refers to an epidemic that has infected many areas of the world nearly simultaneously.

One of the deadliest pandemics to infect the world occurred in 1918. The disease was influenza, but it was unlike any flu anyone had ever seen before. There are three remarkable things about the influenza pandemic of 1918.

The first is that this virus killed between 20 million and 40 million people worldwide in little more than a year. Some estimates put the figure even higher. The real number will never be known because the records of the time are far from accurate.

The second remarkable thing is that this flu is hardly ever mentioned anywhere. Few history textbooks discuss it. People who lived through it were close-mouthed about it for years. News publications printed after the pandemic relegated it to their back pages, if they included it at all.

The third and most frightening thing is that this lethal disease—a disease that often killed its victims in a matter of hours, that spread like wildfire across the entire globe—will in all likelihood return in some form someday.

A miner uses "anti-flu" gargle to ward off the disease.

This book aims to shed light on a little-known episode of world history. By understanding what happened once, we may be able to anticipate and prevent it from happening again. Scientists are working hard to ensure that we can, but it remains to be seen if their efforts will prove successful.

❦

WHAT IS INFLUENZA?

❧

Until proof to the contrary is forthcoming
it must be assumed that the epidemic represented
a very virulent form of the same disease which has spread
throughout the world from time to time for many centuries.
—New York State Department of Health,
post-1918 flu epidemic

FROM NOVEMBER TO APRIL EACH YEAR, thousands of people in the Northern Hemisphere are bedridden with a disease called influenza, or the flu, as it is commonly known. The flu is a respiratory infection. It strikes suddenly and often without warning. Symptoms include high fever, headache, extreme tiredness, dry cough, sore throat, congestion, and body aches.

The flu is caused by the influenza virus. A virus is a submicroscopic agent made up of a protective shell of proteins surrounding the virus's genetic material. Viruses are parasitic, meaning they cannot reproduce without a host body. A virus typically enters a host body through the nose or mouth, when

Opposite:

A hot drink and warm fire are no match for the flu virus.

1

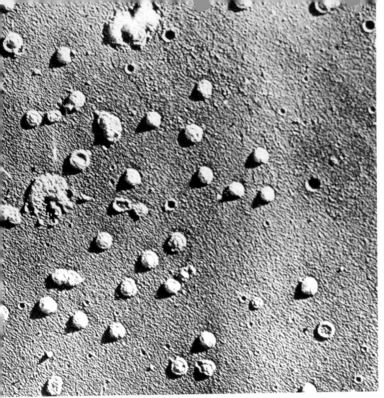

The influenza virus, magnified 60,000 times

the person inhales or ingests material contaminated with the virus.

Once the virus has successfully entered a body, it seeks out cells to help it reproduce. When it finds an appropriate cell, the virus attaches itself to the cell membrane. Then the virus's protective shell makes a hole in the membrane through which the virus injects its genetic material. Once inside, the genetic material takes over the cell and forces it to make copies of the virus. The cell bursts when it can no longer contain all the copies, showering nearby cells with the virus—and the process begins again.

The virus that causes influenza is highly communicable. Symptoms begin one to four days after the virus has invaded the body. Patients are contagious before symptoms develop and stay contagious until all symptoms have disappeared. When a sick person coughs, sneezes, or even speaks, he or she sends millions of virus-laden particles into the air. Whoever inhales those particles can catch the flu. It is also possible to catch the flu by touching an object, such as a doorknob or telephone, that has flu virus on it, then touching your nose or mouth. Frequent hand washing with warm soapy water can help reduce a person's risk of catching the flu this way.

However, the best means of stopping the flu is to isolate anyone with the sickness. People with the flu should stay home from school or work and keep away from social gatherings until all symptoms disappear. Otherwise, they might give the flu to others, who in turn might pass it to more people, and so on.

There is no cure for the flu. Doctors usually recommend getting plenty of rest, drinking lots of liquids, and taking an over-the-counter medication to help temporarily relieve the symptoms. Most people are laid up for one to two weeks. However, in the United States alone, more than 100,000 people every year are hospitalized with flu complications such as pneumonia, and an average of 20,000 people die of such complications. The elderly, the very young, and people with weakened immune systems or chronic health problems such as asthma are typically at greatest risk.

Although there is no cure for the flu, there is a way of preventing infection. Each year researchers develop flu vaccines. Vaccines are substances made of live or dead viruses that are injected into the body. The body reacts to the virus's invasion by creating antibodies that attack and destroy the virus. These antibodies remain in the body for years after infection, ready to attack should the virus invade again.

However, the influenza virus is very tricky. It mutates, or changes, frequently. Flu vaccines created for one year are not necessarily effective for the next flu season. People must get a new "flu shot" at the start of each flu season or risk getting sick. And even then they may not be fully protected, because the flu vaccine is only 60 to 70 percent effective. However, people who have been vaccinated and contract the flu usually have milder symptoms than those who haven't received the shot.

Flu viruses infect many species, including chickens, horses, and pigs.

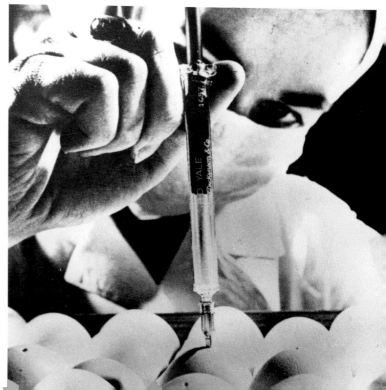

New flu vaccines are manufactured each year.

THE CHANGEABLE INFLUENZA VIRUS

The influenza virus is one of the most changeable viruses to plague humankind. Scientists identify three main categories of influenza virus: Type A, Type B, and Type C. All three cause the flu in humans. However, Type C usually causes only a mild respiratory illness and is not believed to be responsible for widespread outbreaks. The winter epidemics that occur annually are caused by Types A and B. People infected with these types suffer more severe symptoms. In fact, as many as 36,000 Americans die every year from influenza caused by Types A and B.

All three types of influenza virus are constantly changing, or mutating. The mutations affect two proteins, hemagglutinin (H) and neuraminidase (N), which are found in the virus's protective shell. Changes occur in two ways. The first is antigenic *drift*. Drift happens constantly and causes the proteins to change little by little until, eventually, the virus has become a new strain. Drift occurs in all three types of virus.

The second way an influenza virus changes is by antigenic *shift*. Shift also affects the proteins of the virus's shell. However, shift occurs only occasionally and, as far as scientists can tell, only to the Type A virus. Changes caused by shift happen very quickly, are very pronounced, and

dramatically alter the appearance of the H and N proteins. Scientists differentiate among Type A mutations by assigning them H and N numbers based on the proteins' appearance. For example, they have identified the most recent kind of flu viruses to infect humans as Type A (H1N1) and Type A (H3N2). Types B and C are not assigned numbers because the changes that occur in them are too subtle to be noteworthy.

Scientists speculate that the influenza pandemic of 1918 was caused by a dramatic shift in the Type A virus. They also believe that a Type A shift caused the 1957–1958 Asian flu, which killed 70,000 Americans, and the Hong Kong flu of 1968–1969, which killed 34,000 Americans. This last strain still exists today.

Fortunately, some cases where shift occurred did not result in epidemics. In 1976 there was an outbreak of swine flu at Fort Dix, New Jersey. (Swine flu got its name because pigs are typically its victims. However, the swine flu virus can also infect humans.) As soldiers at Fort Dix fell ill, the experts warned that the outbreak could turn into an epidemic. A vaccine was developed and injected into more than 40 million Americans. Luckily, the virus didn't spread.

These animals can get the same flu symptoms, and experience the same lethal results, as humans. Some species, however, can be completely asymptomatic. Wild birds in particular often show no sign of illness, yet they can carry as many as twenty-two strains of influenza in their intestines. It is rare for a human to catch the flu from an infected animal, but it can happen.

THE HISTORY OF INFLUENZA

No one is really sure where the influenza virus originated or how long it has been infecting humans. The first recorded outbreaks of the flu occurred in Europe in the years 1510, 1557, and 1580. The last of these outbreaks reached epidemic proportions, although the exact mortality rate is not known.

The disease was first called influenza during a pandemic in 1781. *Influenza* is Italian for "influence." In the eighteenth century, many people believed that human health was influenced by the heavens. When a person got sick, it was because the planets, stars, moon, and sun were having a bad influence upon the body.

Up until the twentieth century, people were stumped in their efforts to explain the cause of influenza. Two pandemics, one in 1847–1848 and another in 1889, were thought to have been caused by miasma, or foul air from a poisonous cloud. The 1889 flu pandemic was called the Chinese distemper because it was supposed to have originated in the dust swirling up from the dry banks of the Yellow River of China.

Despite its frequent appearances throughout the world, the rapidity with which it spread, and the fact that it was capable of causing death, influenza was rarely looked upon with dread. Why?

Opposite: Vaccination helps the immune system fight off different mutations of flu virus.

It may be that the symptoms of the flu, unlike other diseases, did not include any terrifying visible signs. Smallpox covered patients with oozing pustules and left survivors horribly disfigured with pockmarks. Leprosy ate away the victims' flesh. Bubonic plague caused the lymph nodes to swell to the size of eggs. Cholera victims had such severe diarrhea that their flesh sank into their skeletons before death. Compared to these symptoms, the aches, fever, and sore throat of flu sufferers undoubtedly seemed mild.

Another possibility is that enough people had suffered through and survived the flu that they came to consider it an inconvenience rather than a threat. When people did die from the disease, it was because they were very old, very young, or weak in the first place. It was possible to accept these deaths as tragic but not extraordinary. Overall, most people regarded the flu as troublesome, not deadly.

Most, but not all. In 1894 a physician wrote an essay that was printed in the *Journal of the American Medical Association.* Influenza was making its way through the United States at the time, but as always it was virtually unnoticed by the medical profession. The writer cautioned doctors to pay more attention: "This disease . . . has not received the consideration it deserves, for it extends throughout the habitable world and has destroyed more lives than the cholera and yellow fever put together."

Many people would soon wish they had paid greater heed to this warning.

THE SPANISH FLU

In 1918 the most lethal strain of influenza ever known raced around the world. Its appearance coincided with the last months of World War I (1914-1918). Different countries called the illness different things. The French called it purulent bronchitis or the grippe. To the Italians, it was sandfly fever. Germans named it lightning catarrh or Flanders fever. And in Japan it was known as wrestler's fever because it could flatten a person with such ease. But the name that has gone down in history is the Spanish flu.

In the summer of 1918 more than eight million people in Spain, or one out of every three, were bedridden by the flu. Even King Alfonso XIII was laid up. Government offices and businesses shut down. Trains and trams stopped running. In short, life paused while the flu took hold.

Word soon spread about Spain's epidemic. Spain had chosen to stay out of World War I. Unlike the countries involved in the war, Spain didn't censor information that was sent overseas. At the height of the flu epidemic, the news network of Spain sent a cable to London alerting the British to the situation: "A Strange Form of Disease of Epidemic Character Has Appeared In Madrid. The Epidemic Is Of A Mild Nature, No Deaths Having Been Reported."

This same strain of flu had been striking other areas of the world, including the United States. However, the disease was given the name Spanish influenza—or Spanish Lady by some—because Spain was the first country to officially recognize it. When people refer to the influenza pandemic of 1918, they usually shorten that name to the "Spanish flu."

The Spanish flu struck the world in three waves. The first wave started in March 1918 and lasted until August. It was mild compared to what was to come. The second and most

King Alfonso XIII of Spain survived the Spanish flu.

lethal wave started only weeks after the first ended. It lasted until mid-November before dying out. The third wave was milder than the second but deadlier than the first. It struck at the year's end and did not die out until the spring of 1919.

In little more than a year, the Spanish flu sickened an unbelievable 2 billion people worldwide. Of those, it killed between 20 million and 40 million. In the United States alone, more than 600,000 people—2 percent of the 1918 population—died.

Meanwhile, World War I was claiming its own victims. Soldiers on both sides died in great numbers, some ripped apart by the newly developed machine guns, others killed by diseases that spread through the trenches along the front lines. The total number of soldiers, sailors, and airmen who died during World War I was 9.2 million.

Doctors treat a flu victim at the U.S. Naval Hospital in New Orleans in 1918.

More than 126,000 of those casualties were Americans, yet only 53,000 died in combat. Disease claimed the lives of the other 73,000 American soldiers. Of those 73,000, 43,000 were killed by the Spanish flu. When this number is added to the domestic tally, the final estimate of Americans who died of the flu comes close to 650,000. That figure is greater than the number of American soldiers killed in World War I, World War II, the Korean War, and the Vietnam War *combined*.

How and why the virus mutated into such a deadly form is a mystery scientists are still trying to unravel. But they know one thing for sure: if it happened once, it can happen again. The question now is, will we be any more prepared to fight a flu epidemic than the doctors, nurses, and caregivers of 1918?

CHAPTER TWO

THE FIRST WAVE

*The number of sick develop[ed] so rapidly
that hospitals were within a day or two so overfull
that fresh admissions were impossible.*
—Dr. Herbert French, British Ministry of Health,
May 1918

S DAWN WAS BREAKING ON MARCH 11, 1918, Private Gitchell, a company cook at Camp Funston in Fort Riley, Kansas, reported that he had a sore throat, fever, headache, and muscle pains. Fort Riley was a newly constructed army base used to train soldiers to fight in World War I. The camp was filled to overflowing with 26,000 recruits. Gitchell was quickly sent to the contagious ward of the camp hospital so that he wouldn't infect his comrades-in-arms.

Less than an hour later, Corporal Lee W. Drake was admitted with the same symptoms. Sergeant Adolph Hurby and two other soldiers followed soon after. By lunchtime, the

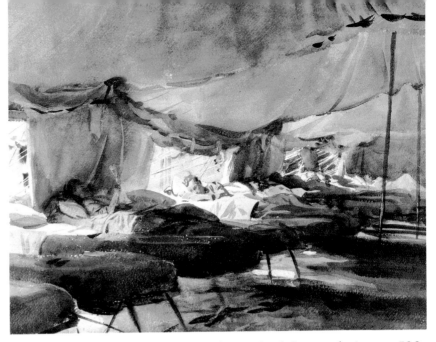

Makeshift hospitals housed hundreds of U.S. soldiers stricken with the flu.

head count was up to 107. By the end of the week, it was 522. Fort Riley was in the midst of a flu epidemic.

The flu raged through the camp for five weeks, bringing normal operations to a near halt. The disease sent 1,127 soldiers to their beds—and 46 to their graves. The deaths were the result of pneumonia brought on by the flu.

Where had the bug come from? Blame was placed on a blinding dust storm that had swept through the area on March 9. Dust storms were common in Kansas, but the conditions at Fort Riley made this particular storm worse than usual.

Fort Riley had a large horse and mule population that produced a great volume of manure. To reduce the volume, soldiers burned the manure, creating piles of ashes and a smoky haze. Those working at or near these fires developed coughs and wheezes. In March high winds kicked up the ashes into huge dust clouds. When the winds died down, a quarter inch of dust settled on everything in the camp. Soldiers cleaning up the dust started coughing as well.

Is it possible that the flu virus started in this dust cloud? Could the virus have somehow been transferred from burned animal droppings to the men? Whether the dust storm was to blame or not, the story that the storm brought on the epidemic has persisted. But if the dust was the cause, how would one explain that even as Fort Riley succumbed to its flu epidemic, army bases and other locations around the United States were also reporting outbreaks?

Camp Kearny in California, Camp Johnson in Florida, Camp Lee in Virginia, Camp McClellan in Alabama, Camp Sevier in South Carolina, and Fort Oglethorpe in Georgia—all had soldiers laid up with the flu during the same weeks that Fort Riley was besieged. The navy, too, experienced outbreaks—as many as 300 cases on ships docked on the East Coast. The Ford Motor Company of Detroit, Michigan, recorded more than 1,000 workers out sick with the flu in March. In April and May, 500 of 1,900 prisoners in San Quentin prison were taken ill.

Although the flu's point of origin is unclear, one thing is certain. The virus didn't stay in one place for long. Wherever sick soldiers traveled, the flu went with them. And with the world embroiled in the First World War, massive numbers of soldiers, sick and healthy, were moving constantly.

THE FIRST WORLD WAR

World War I was unlike any conflict ever witnessed before. It began with a single gunshot and ended with millions of casualties.

On June 28, 1914, Archduke Franz Ferdinand, heir to the throne of Austria-Hungary, was assassinated. His death sparked the start of the Great War, as it was called. On July 28, 1914, Austria-Hungary declared war on Serbia, claiming that the Serbian government was behind the assassination. From there, other countries fell into the war like dominoes falling in a line. Germany aligned with Austria-Hungary and began a quest for domination in Europe. France, Great Britain, and Russia sided with Serbia, making up the core of the Allied forces. Within months, much of the world was divided.

Many expected that the Great War would be one of massive movement, with offensive attacks pushing one or the other side farther into enemy territory. Instead, the war became a defensive one, a war of attrition rather than a war of aggression. The primary reason for this was the introduction of new weapons and ways of fighting.

The most important new weapon was the machine gun. The machine gun could fire as many as eighty shots a minute, far outstripping the rifle's three or four. No longer could infantrymen rush enemy troops and overcome them with superior numbers. If they tried, they were cut down by bullets from a few carefully placed machine guns.

Other new weapons added their own brand of destructive power. Tanks roared across the war-torn landscapes. Poisonous gas from chemical weapons shrouded the air with noxious fumes. Long-range shells launched from modern, easily transported cannons exploded on distant targets.

In order to withstand attacks by these new weapons, soldiers dug systems of trenches that allowed them to remain below ground level and more or less out of harm's way. These trenches stretched in broken lines for miles, with the trenches of Germany and the other Central Powers facing off against those of the Allied forces. These face-to-face trench systems made up the front lines of the war. The area between the trenches was known as no-man's-land.

Soldiers lived in trenches for long stretches of time. Conditions were far from ideal. Enemy fire constantly threatened. The men were at the mercy of the weather. Mud and filth were constant companions, as were rodents, fleas, and lice. Disease was common and traveled freely up and down the lines and across no-man's-land.

The United States entered the war in April 1917, prompted into action by German acts of aggression. The first U.S. troops were sent overseas in June. During the following months, hundreds of thousands of young American men joined the war effort. They trained at camps like Fort Riley, then were mobilized and shipped off across the Atlantic, bringing to the war new strength, new supplies, and a determination to defeat the enemy.

In May 1918 they also started bringing the flu.

THE FIRST WAVE WASHES OVER THE WORLD

Details of just how much devastation was caused by the first wave of the Spanish flu are sketchy. In 1918 physicians and city officials were not required to record cases of influenza. The few existing records indicate that the virus reached far and wide during the spring and summer months of 1918.

An outbreak occurred in April aboard a ship carrying the U.S. Fifteenth Cavalry. Thirty-six members of this unit were stricken by flu. Six died of complications.

Trenches protected soldiers from flying bullets, but not disease.

French citizens welcome American soldiers—and the flu—in Saint-Nazaire.

Influenza soon turned up in several places in Europe. In one area its first occurrence coincided with the arrival of American troops trained at Fort Riley. The Ninety-second Division of the American Expeditionary Force (AEF) disembarked in Brest and Saint-Nazaire, France, in early May. Both towns were beset by influenza midmonth. The disease then traveled by train with the soldiers, reaching the AEF's headquarters in Chaumont. One hundred thirty-two cases were recorded there in twelve days.

As American soldiers mingled with the French military personnel, they passed on the disease. Soon much of the French army was in the grip of the grippe, as they called it. Officers of the French military command were so alarmed by the numbers of sick that they issued an order for all flu cases to be reported to them by telegraph.

Meanwhile, the virus was rapidly showing up in other parts of Europe. Every cough, sneeze, or wheeze of a sick soldier helped spread the contagion. The Royal Navy of Great Britain had 10,313 flu cases by mid-May. Italy and Spain were infected in May as well. (It was during this time that Spain sent the telegram that earned the flu its name.) In June the British army had an estimated 31,000 cases, six times more than those recorded a month earlier. Scotland listed 107 deaths from pneumonia caused by flu in one week. Italy and Spain were all but crippled by the disease.

Because most of the public was focused on the war, the first wave of the flu received little attention. Still, some medical professionals took notice. Dr. Herbert French sent a report of his misgivings to the British Ministry of Health:

> In the midst of perfect health, in a circumscribed community, such as a barracks or a school, the first case of influenza would occur, and then within the next few hours or days a large proportion—and occasionally every single individual of that community—would be stricken down. . . . The patient would be seized rapidly, or almost suddenly, with a sense of such prostration as to be utterly unable to carry on with what he might be doing; from sheer lassitude he would be obliged to lie down where he was, or crawl with difficulty back to bed.

In general, however, the flu was seen as a nuisance rather than a real threat to public or military safety—even when the "three-day fever," as many soldiers called the disease, postponed or shut down the normal activity of the armies. The British Royal Navy couldn't put to sea for nearly three weeks in May because so many of its sailors were sick. Likewise, some American ships and submarines halted their voyages, reporting that as many as half of their personnel were laid up. The British had planned an attack against a German stronghold in La Becque, France, on June 30. The attack was postponed because too many soldiers were down with the flu.

Meanwhile, the virus had jumped across no-man's-land into Germany. "It was a grievous business," wrote German General Erich Ludendorff in a memo, "having to listen every morning to the Chiefs of Staff's recital of the number of influenza cases, and their complaints about the weakness of their troops."

Ludendorff blamed the flu for the failure of a crucial offensive in July. The aim of this attack was to pin the left wing of the Allied troops against the southern coast of the English Channel. Many historians speculate that if this attack had been successful, Germany might have won the war.

The Spanish flu traveled beyond western Europe throughout the spring and summer of 1918. Soldiers helped bring it to areas that otherwise might not have been affected because of their distance from the initial outbreaks. North Africa was struck in May. India, Japan, China, and the Philippines were infected in June. That same month, before moving on to Hawaii, the epidemic broke out in Cuba, Puerto Rico, and the area around the Panama Canal. In July, Russia fell victim; New Zealand followed in August.

By midsummer the virus had all but run its course through the military. Now it started to strike civilians in full force. Records from London show that 700 people died of the flu and another 475 of pneumonia in July alone. An estimated 53,000 cases were reported in Switzerland that same month. Copenhagen, Denmark, and Christiania (now Oslo), Norway, logged a combined total of 14,000 cases in the middle two weeks of the month. Pneumonia and flu claimed 214 lives in Hamburg, Germany.

July marked the worst month of the first wave of the Spanish flu. In August the number of cases dwindled, then died out. Tens of thousands of people had died worldwide, and millions more had been sickened. Yet influenza made few headlines. For most people, World War I overshadowed everything else. In many countries, censorship concealed the truth about the pandemic, lest it cause a panic.

U.S. servicemen in France wore masks to protect against the flu.

A LULL IN THE STORM

Historians look back at the first wave with interest because they know that it was merely a precursor of the horrors that were to follow. In addition, they note two intriguing facts. First, when looking at a map of areas affected by this wave, they see that after the initial outbreaks in the army camps, the United States was practically unaffected by the pandemic. The flu failed to take hold even when the disease was reintroduced to U.S. ports by ships carrying sick passengers. That's probably because enough people living near the ports had acquired immunity to the disease during the spring outbreaks. With few susceptible hosts, the virus died out before it could penetrate inland.

The second and much more chilling fact about the first wave was that the virus had deviated from its usual killing

Soldiers, weakened by the horrific living conditions of the trenches, fell victim to the flu by the thousands.

pattern. When plotted on a graph, flu deaths generally make a U shape—peaks at each end of the age scale, with much lower numbers in the middle age ranges. In this case the flu deaths made a W shape. The virus still killed children and the elderly, but it also claimed the lives of young soldiers and civilians.

Although many soldiers during the summer of 1918 were malnourished, exhausted, and living in unsanitary environments, they were nonetheless in the prime of their lives. It is not surprising that they were stricken with the flu, given the less-than-perfect living conditions. But the fact that so many became gravely ill instead of only mildly sick—and that civilians of the same age range were affected similarly—should perhaps have raised a few eyebrows. However, it did not.

The authorities of the time can't be blamed for turning their backs on the spring and summer wave of influenza. They were so busy with the daily upheaval caused by the war that they had little time to devote to people with the sniffles. When the pandemic died down in August, they closed the slim volume on influenza, never suspecting that a new, more deadly chapter would soon be written.

THE SECOND WAVE

I had a little bird
Its name was Enza.
I opened the window
And In-flu-enza.
—Children's jump-rope rhyme popular in 1918

AT THE END OF AUGUST 1918, Spanish influenza resurfaced. Three towns—Freetown, Sierra Leone; Brest, France; and Boston, Massachusetts—were stricken almost simultaneously.

Freetown, a port on the coast of West Africa, produced coal during World War I. Military ships frequently stopped there to take on coal. On August 15, 1918, the HMS *Mantua* out of Great Britain docked in Freetown. Two hundred of the sailors on board had mild cases of the flu. The virus soon jumped from the sailors to the residents of Freetown.

The first Freetown cases were noted on August 24. Three days later, five hundred out of six hundred workers from the

Sierra Leone Coaling Company failed to report for work. Within a month, two-thirds of the inhabitants of Sierra Leone had contracted the disease.

The virus was no longer the mild form that had inconvenienced the crewmen of the *Mantua*, however. In Freetown alone, more than one thousand people—an estimated 3 percent of the population—died of the deadly strain and its complications. Scientists today speculate that the virus must have mutated after the first wave, since it caused more fatal infections when it resurfaced. Yet, as time would show, many people who had been infected in the first wave were immune to the deadlier strain. This seems to indicate that the virus was still close enough to its original form to be recognized and fended off by the antibodies of those people's immune systems.

Whatever the case, the newer, deadlier strain soon spread beyond Sierra Leone. With so many coal laborers sick, ships docking in Freetown were forced to put their sailors to work loading coal. These same sailors brought the mutated flu virus aboard their vessels. Once on board, it spread quickly, and sometimes with deadly results. On one ship, the HMS *Africa*, 75 percent of the personnel were taken ill and fifty-one crew members died.

Brest, France, was the second place the flu resurfaced in the late summer of 1918. Brest, a major seaport, was an important site of disembarkation for the American troops. On August 22 the flu sailed into port, carried either by soldiers arriving from the United States or by Frenchmen coming in to begin training. By September 15, at least 1,350 people had been hospitalized with the flu. Of those, 370 died.

Meanwhile, an ocean away, the flu was taking hold in Boston, Massachusetts.

Soldiers and the flu disembarked in Brest, France, in August 1918.

THE FLU HITS BOSTON

Commonwealth Pier in Boston was a launching pad from which troops were shipped overseas. The pier housed anywhere from 3,500 to 7,000 men in a barracks called the Receiving Ship. The Receiving Ship was not an actual ship, but rather a holding station for soldiers and sailors on their way to war. It was hardly a comfortable place to stay. It was overcrowded, overrun with rats, and short of soap, drinking fountains, and properly working toilets. It was in this inhospitable space that troops awaited transfer to their next post. This was also where the second wave of the Spanish flu first struck in the Western Hemisphere.

The first flu cases on Commonwealth Pier were reported on August 27. Eight more appeared the next day, and fifty-eight the day after that. Within a week, more than three hundred men were sick. The medical facilities of Commonwealth Pier couldn't handle them all. Fifty men were transferred to Chelsea Naval Hospital the first week of September. Within two days, two military officers stationed at that hospital were sick.

To those keeping an eye on the disease and the general health of the soldiers, it seemed likely that the flu would soon spread even further unless precautions were taken.

Dr. William M. Bryan was the U.S. Public Health Service officer for the First Naval District of Boston. He was appalled by the conditions at the Receiving Ship and by how quickly the flu was making its way through the ranks. "The congestion of the ship," Bryan wrote, "as well as the repeated intercourse with the civilian population is believed to be a menace to the health of the personnel, and may have its influence upon the present prevalence of influenza." It is interesting that Bryan considered the spread of the disease to be from civilians to soldiers, not the other way around. Regardless, his advice that soldiers and civilians stay separated was sound. It was also largely ignored.

The Massachusetts Department of Health also showed concern about the spread of the disease. In an article in the *Boston Globe*, it warned that "unless precautions are taken the disease in all probability will spread to the civilian population."

Lieutenant Junior Grade J. J. Keegan, a medical officer in Boston, was of the opinion that the disease would "spread rapidly across the entire country, attacking between 30 and 40 percent of the population, and running an acute course in from four to six weeks in each community."

But these words of warning fell largely on deaf ears. Precautions that might have helped stem the contagion— quarantining the sick, postponing public events, and informing the public about the health hazard—never materialized. In fact, soldiers and civilians continued to mingle regularly.

On September 3, in the midst of the epidemic at the

Receiving Ship, Boston held a "Win the War for Freedom" parade. Four thousand people took part, including one thousand soldiers from Commonwealth Pier. That same day, the first civilian was hospitalized with the flu. On September 5 thousands of civilians and soldiers attended the dedication of a new building for Harvard's Navy Radio School. They listened to speeches, then dined and danced until past midnight.

Within days of these events, the flu had spread throughout the city of Boston. The first casualties—a civilian, a navy sailor, and a member of the merchant marines—died on September 8. By mid-September, William C. Woodward, the health commissioner of Boston, estimated that more than three thousand people had been hospitalized with the flu. On September 18 alone, forty people died.

The flu was not content to stay within the city limits. Even as it raged in Boston, it also made its way to Portsmouth, New Hampshire; Newport, Rhode Island; and Fort Devens, an army base thirty miles west of Boston.

A child, one of countless civilian flu victims, languishes in bed.

FORT DEVENS

Fort Devens was a training camp designed to house 35,000 soldiers. In September 1918 it had more than 45,000. The flu couldn't have found a better breeding ground than the overcrowded army camp. The first cases were reported on September 8. Within a few days, an uncontrollable epidemic had broken out. All activity halted as new cases piled up. By the middle of the month, the camp's hospital staff couldn't handle the load and called for help.

The U.S. surgeon general ordered William Henry Welch, one of the country's most prominent doctors, to Fort Devens. Welch and his colleagues had recently inspected a number of army camps around the country. They had seen their share of sickness among soldiers in the past months, and in the course of their careers they had witnessed widespread disease throughout the ranks. But what they saw at Fort Devens was more horrifying than anything they had ever come across.

Dr. William Henry Welch could not prevent the ghastly deaths at Fort Devens.

The flu started out in much the same way the disease always had, with sore throats, coughs, fevers, and aches. But from there it often took a deadly turn. Patients gasped for breath. Bloody foam erupted from their noses and mouths. Their skin turned blue-black. Then they died, sometimes within twenty-four hours of first falling ill.

On the day before Welch arrived, sixty-six men had died of pneumonia brought on by this new, lethal flu. On the day of his arrival, another sixty-three succumbed. And the numbers continued to mount each day of the epidemic.

Years later, Colonel Victor C. Vaughan, a doctor accompanying Welch, wrote about what he saw: "[There are] hundreds of stalwart young men in the uniform of their country coming into the wards of the hospital in groups of ten or more. They are placed on the cots until every bed is full yet others crowd in. Their faces soon wear a bluish cast; a distressing cough brings up the blood stained sputum. In the morning the dead bodies are stacked about the morgue like cord wood. This picture was painted on my memory cells."

Another doctor, known to historians only as Roy, left a similar picture in a letter he wrote to a friend on September 29: "[The soldiers] rapidly develop the most viscous [thick, sticky] type of Pneumonia that has ever been seen. Two hours after admission they have the Mahogany spots over the cheek bones, and a few hours later you can begin to see the Cyanosis extending from their ears and spreading all over the face. . . . It is only a matter of a few hours then until death comes and it is simply a struggle for air until they suffocate. It is horrible. One can stand to see one, two or twenty men die, but . . . we have been averaging about 100 deaths per day."

The rapidly spreading disease was not the only problem. As the death count mounted, so did the bodies. "It takes Special trains to carry away the dead," Roy wrote. "For several days there were not coffins and the bodies piled up something fierce and we used to go down to the morgue and look at the boys laid out in long rows."

The doctors knew the disease was something highly unusual. Even so, they were unprepared for what they discovered when they began to perform autopsies. When they opened up the chest cavities, they expected to see some damage to the lungs, since influenza is a respiratory infection and since so many of the dead had struggled to breathe at the end. Lungs are normally very lightweight, filled with tiny air sacs. What the doctors saw in the victims' lungs shocked them.

The diseased lungs were dense masses of flesh, soaked like wet sponges with frothy, blood-stained fluid. This fluid had replaced the oxygen in the soldiers' lungs. The men had literally drowned in the liquid in their lungs.

Welch, Vaughan, and the other doctors were shaken. They had never seen a disease attack the body in such a way, or with such virulence. "This must be some new kind of infection," one doctor remembered Welch saying. "Or plague."

Welch did not use the word *plague* lightly, and the other physicians knew it. As Dr. Rufus Cole said later, "It shocked me to find that the situation, momentarily at least, was too much even for Doctor Welch."

During the course of these horrifying autopsies, the doctors sliced off bits of lung tissue, preserved them in paraffin wax, and sent them to the National Tissue Repository in Washington, D.C. Other doctors on other army bases were performing similar procedures. In all, seventy lung samples were sent to the repository for later examination. However, because the war had such a claim on the medical profession, these samples remained untouched and unstudied.

THE FLU SPREADS

The epidemic raged at Fort Devens until the end of October. Seventeen thousand people, including more than one hundred nurses caring for the sick, were stricken. Seven hundred eighty-seven people died.

Compared to the numbers that were dying on the battlefields of France, these figures were small. Had the flu been isolated at Fort Devens, it would have registered as only a blip, if at all. But the flu was not content to stay put.

It raced like wildfire throughout Massachusetts, sickening as many as 85,000 in September and prompting Lieutenant Governor Calvin Coolidge to telegram neighboring states

with requests for additional doctors and nurses. But by this time, most medically trained people were either overseas fighting the war or busy with flu epidemics in their own areas. In the region from New Hampshire to Virginia, deaths from flu in August were estimated at 2,800; in September, that number skyrocketed to 12,000.

Military training camps across the country were so hard hit that many were placed under quarantine. At the end of September the provost marshal general of the United States cancelled the October draft. The draft would have called up 142,000 men—men desperately needed in Europe. But the risk of exposing new recruits to the virus, and further spreading the killer disease by moving them around the country, was just too great.

Doctors were in short supply in the United States during the flu epidemic.

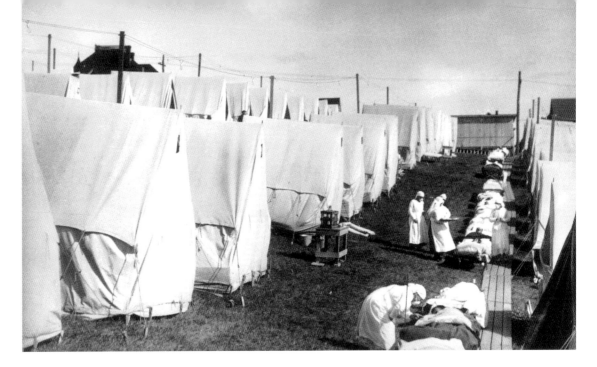

Canvas tents served as hospital rooms for hundreds of Massachusetts flu patients in October 1918.

Yet nothing anyone did seemed to make any difference. The flu swept on, striking military posts and major cities almost simultaneously. Philadelphia was one of the hardest hit. The statistics of sick and dead there are staggering.

THE FLU IN PHILADELPHIA

At the end of August and the beginning of September, Philadelphia was surrounded by pockets of flu. Fort Dix in New Jersey and Fort Meade in Maryland were both experiencing outbreaks, as was the naval yard in Philadelphia itself.

City officials took some measures to control the disease. They launched a campaign to stop public spitting, sneezing, and coughing, and passed a law that made influenza a reportable disease.

Yet at the same time, they made announcements that led the population to believe that it was safe from influenza. Health officials claimed that the flu was dying out in the armed forces and wouldn't reach civilians. They told the public that the cause of the Spanish flu had been discovered.

It was supposedly a bacterium known as Pfeiffer's bacillus, and a cure, they said, was being developed.

Such heartening reports may have encouraged people to let down their guard. In any case, the flu had found a vulnerable population, one with plenty of hosts. The virus took hold and didn't let go for many weeks.

People were urged to help fight the war by fighting the spread of infection.

The first cases of Spanish flu in Philadelphia occurred on September 12. On September 28 the city held a Liberty Loan Drive, a public event designed to raise money for the war effort. Two hundred thousand people attended the festivities. A few days later, Philadelphia registered 635 new cases of the flu. That number increased daily.

City officials realized they were in the midst of an epidemic. They shut down schools and public meeting places and closed churches and theaters. They ordered people to wear gauze masks, which many believed could stop the flu, when in public—all in an attempt to stem the spread of the disease. It soon became obvious that such measures were fruitless.

The first week of October saw 706 die of the flu. By October 12 the death toll was 2,635. A week later, the count

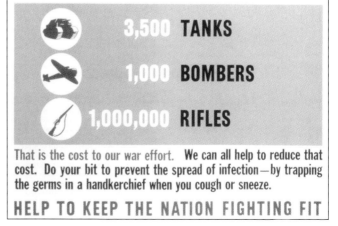
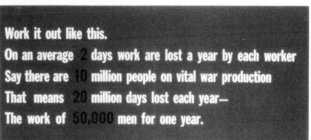

THE COST OF THE COMMON COLD & INFLUENZA

Work it out like this.
On an average 2 days work are lost a year by each worker
Say there are 10 million people on vital war production
That means 20 million days lost each year—
The work of 50,000 men for one year.

★ IF one third of all the men and women who lost these days were making tanks, one third bombers, and one third rifles
Then in that time they could make

3,500 TANKS

1,000 BOMBERS

1,000,000 RIFLES

That is the cost to our war effort. We can all help to reduce that cost. Do your bit to prevent the spread of infection—by trapping the germs in a handkerchief when you cough or sneeze.

HELP TO KEEP THE NATION FIGHTING FIT

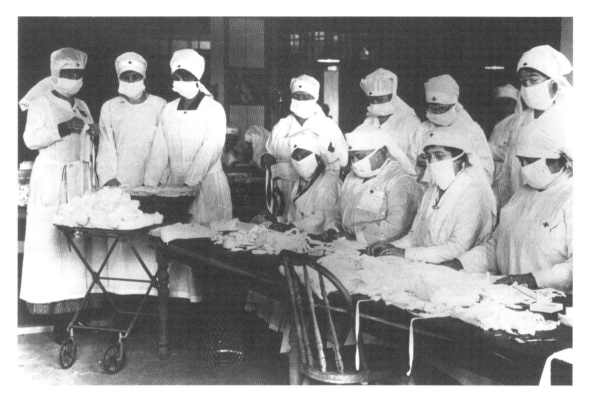

had risen to 4,597. By the first week of November, when the flu finally seemed to be slowing, the number of dead had nearly tripled to a staggering 12,162. On one day alone—October 10—759 Philadelphians died of influenza and pneumonia.

Thousands of sick people flooded the hospitals. They couldn't have found a worse time to seek medical attention. Many of Philadelphia's doctors and nurses were overseas contributing to the war effort. Those remaining were overwhelmed by the number of patients—and soon, by the number of dead.

"As their lungs filled . . . the patients became short of breath and increasingly cyanotic," wrote Isaac Starr, a third-year medical student at the University of Pennsylvania in 1918. "After gasping for several hours they became delirious and incontinent, and many died struggling to clear their airways of a blood-tinged froth that sometimes gushed from their nose and mouth. It was a dreadful business."

There were instances in which whole families succumbed to the disease. Children were orphaned overnight as first one parent died, then the other. In some cases the sick lay alongside the dead until someone from outside the household happened to check on them. Volunteers, many of them women, tried their best to give comfort and aid—knowing that each time they visited a sickbed they were putting their own health, and possibly their lives, at risk.

At the height of the epidemic, Philadelphia's undertakers couldn't keep up with the body count. They ran out of coffins, spaces to put coffins with bodies in them, and places to bury the victims. Embalmers were in such short supply that many bodies started to rot. Horse carts trolled the city streets, their drivers calling for the dead to be brought out. Steam shovels dug trenches in which to bury the poor, while volunteers and prisoners from the House of Detention dug individual graves for those who could afford them.

Many businesses and services were severely affected by shortages of labor. The telephone company issued the following appeal in newspapers:

"Telephone Service Faces a Crisis: The situation is one which the public must meet squarely—800 operators—27% of our force—are now absent due to the influenza. It is every person's duty to the community to cut out every call that is not absolutely necessary that the essential needs of the government, doctors, and nurses may be cared for."

Some businesses responded to the city's call for help by

closing shop and distributing food and other supplies to those in need. One department store donated two trucks to be used as ambulances. Another used its telephone line to take calls from flu victims.

By the end of November the flu had finally run its course in Philadelphia. The number of fatalities was staggering, but even more shocking was the fact that the virus had killed such a huge number of people between the ages of twenty-five and thirty-four—a section of the population that normally survived the flu. As most people were discovering, this flu was anything but normal.

THE FLU IN SAN FRANCISCO

The West Coast had more or less escaped the first wave of the flu in the spring. According to authorities, the second wave was beginning to die down in other parts of the country. Therefore, many people living on the West Coast believed that the deadly flu would never reach them. They were wrong.

As on the East Coast, the flu struck the military first. Camp Lewis in Washington State reported 173 cases on September 20. On September 23 more than 10,000 civilians visited the camp to see the review of the National Guard infantry. Two days later, the flu broke out in Seattle in epidemic proportions.

The first case of flu in San Francisco was reported on September 24. The patient was Edward Wagner, a young man who had recently moved from Chicago. He was hospitalized, and his house was placed under quarantine.

Four days after Wagner was hospitalized, San Francisco held a Liberty Loan Drive. Ten thousand people attended.

That same week, a crowd of 16,000 gathered at another war rally to hear the popular actress Mary Pickford speak. On October 6, 150,000 people paraded in front of movie cameras at Golden Gate Park for three hours, making a film for their loved ones abroad. On October 11 another 50,000 attended a concert given by tenor Lucien Muratore on behalf of the war effort.

A rally led by Mary Pickford probably helped spread the flu in San Francisco.

The people who attended these gatherings were greatly moved by feelings of patriotism. Many of them were also touched by the flu virus.

By October 14, 991 cases of Spanish flu had been recorded in the San Francisco area; more than one-third of the cases were reported that very day. Five days later, the number of new cases had risen to more than 4,000. One hundred thirty people had died. That number would skyrocket before the disease had run its course.

San Francisco followed Philadelphia's lead and closed schools, theaters, and amusement parks. It forbade church services. People were urged to avoid sneezing and coughing in public and to stay away from anyone who had a respiratory illness. All cases of flu were to be reported.

Citizens were ordered by law to wear gauze masks. "Obey the laws, and wear the gauze. Protect your jaws from septic paws," said a popular rhyme. Those who didn't wear their masks were fined or jailed. In the end, however, such measures proved no more effective in San Francisco than they had in Philadelphia.

San Francisco officials tried to organize a system for getting aid to people. They divided the city into districts, then assigned each district an allotment of doctors, nurses, hospital space, and use of transportation. But the flu didn't follow the lines the authorities had drawn. Some of the poorer sections, including those where large immigrant populations lived in close quarters, were much harder hit than less crowded areas of the city. The numbers and boundaries of districts changed again and again as officials tried to adjust to the needs of the people, but overall the system failed.

Shortages of doctors, nurses, and hospital space contributed to this failure. One overworked and overwrought doctor recalled seeing 525 patients in one day. This doctor had a friend drive him from house to house, but he didn't bother to get into the car. Instead, he balanced on the running board with his medical kit and jumped off when his friend slowed in front of an infected household.

Emergency hospitals were set up in all available large, dry buildings. The Civic Auditorium alone held three hundred beds, all of which were filled during the epidemic's peak. The San Francisco Red Cross was likewise overwhelmed. It could handle only half of the calls it received; at one point, it issued the following appeal:

WEEKLY INFANT DEATH RATE PER 1000 LIVING BIRTHS   WEEKLY DEATH RATE PER 1000 POPULATION

"Women of San Francisco. We Beseech Your Help. You Can Save as Many Lives Today in San Francisco as You Could in France. The Afflicted—Children, Men, Women, The Breadwinners of the Family—Are Calling for Your Merciful Ministrations."

As more people sickened, services floundered. The telephone company begged citizens to make only emergency calls. Seven policemen had died and many more were too sick to work. Nearly one hundred firefighters were laid low. So many of the city's garbage collectors were sick that refuse accumulated in huge stinking piles all over the city. Although this problem was solved temporarily by covering the garbage with dirt, the mounds were constant reminders of the city's crisis.

The epidemic waned in the middle weeks of November. The sick had numbered 23,639 and the dead 2,122 in the

With a graph showing a spike in death rates in the background, women line up to volunteer as caregivers during the epidemic.

fifty-nine days the epidemic had raged. On November 21 sirens were sounded to let people know that it was safe to remove their masks. Life began to resume its normal course—or so people thought.

Two weeks after the sirens wailed, the flu reappeared, possibly brought into the city by new troops stationed outside the San Francisco Bay area. Five thousand new cases were reported in December. When the epidemic had finally run its course once and for all at the end of January, the total number of reported cases was nearly 50,000, and the body count had reached close to 3,500.

Across the nation, people from all walks of life took measures to keep the flu from spreading. Here a street sweeper in New York City keeps his face covered with a mask.

ELSEWHERE IN THE UNITED STATES

Cities and military bases were not the only areas stricken by the Spanish flu. Although the flu took longer to reach remote corners of the country, it had a devastating effect on a number of small communities. Some places were nearly wiped clean of any living human.

The village of Brevig is located on the Seward Peninsula of Alaska. The nearest town is Nome, ninety miles away. In 1918 the only way to reach Brevig from Nome was by dogsled. In late November two visitors from Nome made the trip. They unknowingly brought a third visitor: the flu virus.

Brevig had a population of eighty before the flu struck. Three days after the visitors from Nome arrived, a woman named Mrs. Neelak died of the flu. Before the epidemic was over, seventy-one other villagers had joined her in the grave.

THE 1918 INFLUENZA PANDEMIC

The scenes of death were horrifying. In one igloo bodies had been torn apart and eaten by starving sled dogs. Another igloo held twenty-five frozen corpses. A third was also filled with the dead—and with three living children who had been forced to remain with their deceased relatives until help arrived.

Burying the Brevig dead proved very difficult. There were few able-bodied men still alive who could dig the graves. In addition, the ground was frozen solid. Steam was pumped into the earth to soften it. Then one mass grave was dug for all who had died.

Cities hoped to stop the flu's spread by disinfecting public places.

The number of deaths in this small Inuit community appear rather insignificant when compared to the final tally of those killed by the flu. But one of the dead, a woman whose name has never been discovered, would one day shed a great deal of light on the virus that struck down so many worldwide.

CHAPTER FOUR

THE END OF THE WAR AND THE FLU

*It has attacked the troops, herded together as they are,
with their poor food, poor accommodation, and poor
medical attention, at the front as well as in the rear.*
—*Michel Corday, a French soldier,
writing about the Spanish flu*

THE EXACT NUMBER OF SOLDIERS killed by the Spanish flu is not known. The Allies' military medical personnel simply didn't have the time or resources to note all the deaths caused by the virus. But enough records do exist to indicate that the figure was in the hundreds of thousands.

Newly arrived recruits, men in training or awaiting assignment, and those stationed in rear areas were often hardest hit, for a number of reasons. First, because they were traveling frequently, they came into contact with a great number of people and were therefore likely to be exposed to the virus. Second, many had not been infected during the first wave in the spring and summer of 1918 and so had not

Opposite:

The flu virus found new victims in the ranks of the crowded, malnourished, and wounded soldiers.

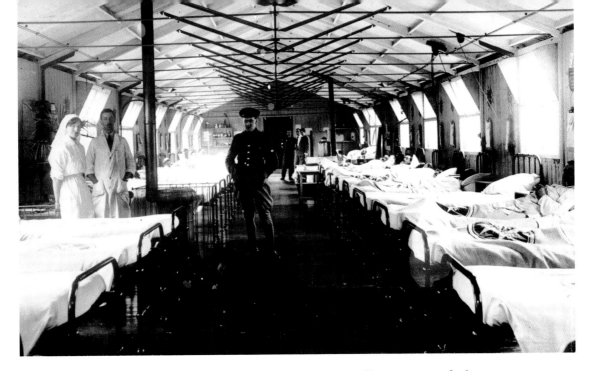

A military hospital
near the front lines.
Most of the beds
were filled with the
wounded rather than
the sick, for soldiers
were reluctant to
report that they
had the flu.

acquired any immunity. Finally, many of these men were exhausted and malnourished, making them prone to infection of all kinds.

Though not as hard hit, the front lines were impacted by the flu as well. One sick man in the trenches could infect others. Even if his comrades remained healthy, his feverish, often delirious condition was a distraction that few of his fellow soldiers in the trenches could afford.

Despite the debilitating effects of the flu, many soldiers failed to report that they were sick. Some feared that they would seem unpatriotic or cowardly, others that they would be separated from their comrades. Still others believed that their absence would leave their side too weakened to win in battle.

In all likelihood, even if those soldiers had reported to army hospitals, they wouldn't have received the care they needed to fight the disease. The medical corps was stretched to the limit tending the unimaginable number of wounded and dead cut down by the twentieth century's new weapons. The addition of thousands of sick men would have made the doctors' and nurses' jobs almost impossible. And these flu cases were all the worse because they were contagious. Wounded men, at least, were no threat to those lying next to them.

The disease raced through the ranks of all countries involved in the war. By late autumn military leaders could no longer ignore the impact it was having on their troops and their ability to fight.

Then, on November 11, 1918, they no longer had to worry about fighting the war. At 11:00 A.M. on that day, Germany signed a general armistice that ended the conflict. The Allied Forces had won.

Celebrations broke out around the world. Masses of people flooded the streets, hugging, kissing, and rejoicing that the awful war that had claimed the lives of so many was finally over.

Within a few weeks of the armistice, the number of reported flu cases fell in many areas of the world. It appeared that the pandemic was also coming to an end. But unlike the war, which was truly over, influenza had one more attack on the way.

THE THIRD WAVE

It is not surprising that the headline news of the war's end relegated the Spanish flu to the back pages. As 1918 turned into 1919, the peace negotiations began in Versailles, France, bumping influenza from the minds of most people altogether—despite the fact that the third and final wave of the pandemic had begun to circle the globe.

Three thousand Parisians died of the flu in December and January. A similar number of deaths occurred in New York City during the same months. San Francisco added more than 1,200 new graves to its cemeteries. Yet none of these deaths, nor the countless others worldwide, registered with the general public—only with those whose loved ones were victims. Although the disease continued to kill throughout the winter and early spring of 1919, few took notice.

Not even the illness of President Woodrow Wilson during the Paris Peace Conference caused more than a quiet stir. Around three o'clock on April 3, 1919, Wilson was suddenly taken sick—so suddenly, in fact, that his physician at first thought he had been poisoned. His temperature rose to 103 degrees. His breathing was labored, and he had a racking cough. For the first twelve hours, his life dangled by a thread.

Fortunately, he survived. Still, many later believed that the president had been forever weakened by his brush with death. When Wilson suffered a debilitating stroke in September 1919, his physician suggested that the lasting effects of the flu were partially to blame. Within a year, Wilson retired from public life.

President Woodrow Wilson, *far right,* contracted the flu during the Paris Peace Conference.

LOOKING BACK

The devastation caused by the double-edged sword of World War I and the Spanish flu was immense. The loss of life had left families destroyed and economies suffering from labor shortages. Emotions, too, were in turmoil, as people mourned the deaths of loved ones.

Yet how these deaths were regarded depended on how the people had died. Young men who had lost their lives on the battlefield, fighting for freedom, were heroes. Somehow, it was easier for the families of these dead to accept their loss, knowing that history would remember the fallen soldiers in a positive light. Those who had died of the flu, however, would receive little recognition. The Spanish influenza itself was barely mentioned in history books or encyclopedias. In less than a decade, it would seem as if the pandemic had never happened.

How could this be? How could people who had lived through one of the world's most lethal epidemics forget what they had seen?

It seems most likely that people simply didn't want to remember. Nightmarish scenes of dead bodies stacked like piles of wood, of young men and women turning blue and gasping for breath, of frustrated doctors and nurses helpless to provide comfort and care—these memories were too painful to recall, and so were pushed away.

In addition, the pandemic was forever linked with the horrors of World War I. It was hard enough to absorb the images of the war without adding those of the flu. If people chose to think of that painful time period at all, most focused on the war, which at least provided the victors with feelings of pride and patriotism.

Finally, the flu may have been easy to forget because there were no lasting reminders of its existence. Those who survived the disease were left intact, with no disfigurement or disability. No world leader had died and left his country in turmoil. The flu virus itself had disappeared.

As if working together in some great silent conspiracy, newspapers, magazines, and other publications written in the years immediately following the pandemic rarely spoke of the flu. Military historians and biographers of the great men and women of World War I usually devoted less than a paragraph to Spanish influenza, and then only to mention the numbers of dead.

Surprisingly, even people in the medical profession chose to turn their backs on the flu. In his memoirs Dr. Victor C. Vaughan gave only a brief description of what he had witnessed of the epidemic at Fort Devens. The pandemic itself received only two lines, as if the doctor knew he could not ignore it completely but wanted nothing more than to forget it: "I am not going into the history of the influenza epidemic. It encircled the globe, visited the remotest corners, taking toll of the most robust, sparing neither soldier nor civilian, and flaunting its red flag in the face of science."

THE FAILURE OF MEDICAL SCIENCE

The medical community may have had another reason for wanting to forget the flu. At no other time in modern history had doctors, nurses, and researchers been so helpless in the face of a disease. Their failure was all the more shocking because of the huge advances made in medicine in the years just before the pandemic.

Medical science, particularly the branch that studied

germs, had grown by leaps and bounds, and the causes of many deadly diseases had been discovered. The microorganisms that caused cholera had been isolated in the 1880s. Bubonic plague bacteria were identified in the next decade. Unsanitary conditions had been connected to the growth and spread of bacteria, leading to campaigns to improve public sanitation and personal hygiene. These advances helped reduce diseases such as cholera, tuberculosis, and typhus to shadows of their former selves.

Every day, it seemed, another drug was developed, another microorganism identified, or another medical miracle performed. People's confidence in the medical profession rose significantly. They came to believe that their doctors would eventually cure them of all illnesses, including the flu.

In 1918 many doctors did believe that the cause of the flu had been discovered and that it was a germ. Dr. Richard Pfeiffer of Germany had isolated bacteria from the lungs of victims of the 1889 influenza pandemic. It was these germs, he theorized, that caused influenza.

When autopsies showed that Pfeiffer's bacillus was present in the lungs of many victims of the 1918 flu, some doctors were convinced it was the cause of the disease. Today we know that is not true. The influenza virus simply made it easier for Pfeiffer's bacillus to infect the lungs, further weakening the patients. But back then, medical researchers were years away from seeing their first virus.

Viruses are submicroscopic. They can only be seen with the aid of an electron microscope. Electron microscopes are much more powerful than light microscopes. The most sophisticated electron microscopes allow the viewer to see particles as small as atoms. However, such microscopes would

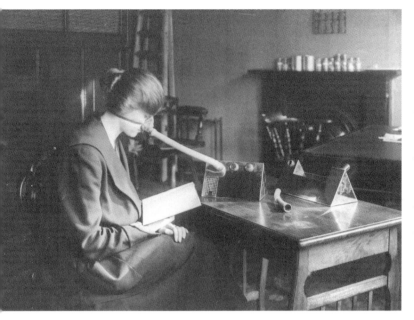

No mask, no matter how "high tech," could stop the submicroscopic flu virus.

not be invented until the 1930s. So during the 1918 pandemic, researchers latched on to the microorganism they could see with their conventional light microscopes—Pfeiffer's bacillus. They performed experiments and developed a vaccine against it. Thousands of people were injected with the new drug; although no one became ill as a result, the vaccine did nothing to stop the flu.

Neither did the gauze masks the public was instructed to wear. Scientists believed gauze masks would keep the flu-causing germ from reaching noses and mouths. But the influenza virus is so small that the gauze was no more capable of blocking it than a tennis racket would be at holding a handful of sand.

Along with the confusion about the cause of the disease, rumors abounded about where it had originated. During the war, many Americans believed that the Germans had unleashed the killer germ as a biological weapon. Lieutenant Colonel Philip S. Doane, head of the health and sanitation section of the Emergency Fleet Corporations, speculated that enemy infiltrators had come ashore from German submarine boats. "It would be quite easy," he said, "for one of these German agents to turn loose Spanish influenza germs in a theater or some place where large numbers of persons are assembled." Others were convinced that a secret German laboratory in Maryland was responsible for sending the germ into the public.

In the absence of sound information and medical advice,

many people turned to folk remedies to avoid the flu. One Pennsylvania woman claimed that she kept her eight children safe by feeding them meals packed with raw onions. Another person recommended rinsing out the mouth with lime water, then inhaling hot water and turpentine fumes to keep the body free of germs. A doctor in Boston proposed

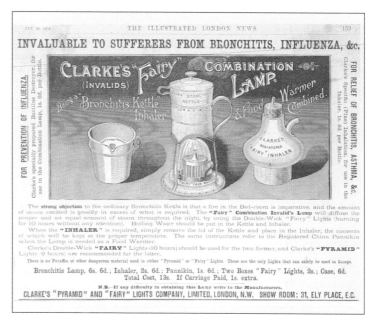

that people go naked because "the skin is a true breathing organ; its millions of blood vessels are forever gasping for air under even the lightest of drapery." Nudity, he believed, would keep germs from being trapped in the body.

Some believed special inhalers relieved the respiratory problems caused by the flu.

Some people wore bags of camphor, an odorous insect repellent, around their necks like pendants. Others carried potatoes in their pockets and tied cucumber slices to their shoes. Some inhaled smoke from wet hay and vapors from alcohol and chloroform. Many bought flu tonics with names such as Grippura and Spanish Influenza Remedy. Some of these preventatives may strike us as comical today, but back then they helped people conquer their fears by giving them the sense that they were doing *something* to help themselves.

As the pandemic finally started to wane in the middle of 1919, the disaster began to slip from the minds of the greater public. Most people were too focused on the process of rebuilding their lives after the war to wonder or worry about a disease that was no longer causing trouble. In the

Gargling was supposed to wash the mouth clean of the flu.

end, only a handful of medical scientists continued to study the Spanish flu.

They had little to work with, however. After Pfeiffer's bacillus was proven not to be the cause of the flu, researchers had to look elsewhere for the culprit. Some believed the disease had been caused by a virus. However, the medical field of virology, the study of viruses, was still very new. In fact, the existence of viruses had only been proven in 1892. That year a Russian botanist named Dmitri Iwanowski performed experiments on tobacco plants. His experiments indicated that a submicroscopic agent had passed through a filter used to trap bacteria and had spread disease to healthy plants.

Other scientists followed up Iwanowski's work, and by the early 1900s most medical researchers had come to accept the existence of viruses—despite the fact that they wouldn't actually see them until the electron microscope was invented. By then, those who wanted to study the 1918 flu couldn't, for the simple fact that the virus no longer existed.

Or did it?

CHAPTER FIVE

THE SEARCH FOR THE KILLER

*Working on the 1918 virus is not just some Sherlock Holmes
work that we're doing because it's a cool thing to do . . . this is not
just a medical detective story. This could happen again.*
—Dr. Jeffrey Taubenberger, pathologist, 1998

IN 1949 A YOUNG MEDICAL STUDENT named Johan V. Hultin began a search for the virus that had killed millions. It was a quest that would take nearly fifty years and the contributions of many scientific minds to complete.

While other scientists had studied influenza in general, Hultin wanted to learn about the 1918 virus in particular. First he had to find a sample of the 1918 killer. He based his search on the theory that samples of the virus could be extracted from the frozen bodies of the Inuit people who had died in Brevig, Alaska. They had lain in the permafrost—permanently frozen ground near the Arctic Circle—for years.

In the early years of flu research, scientists disinfected their clothes to prevent accidental outbreaks.

Would the bodies still contain the virus?

Hultin headed north to Alaska. In June 1951, after weeks of negotiations with Brevig's tribal elders, he received permission to dig up the graves of the victims.

The first body he unearthed was that of a little girl. He carefully took samples of her lung tissue and returned with them to his lab in Iowa. For more than a month, he and other researchers tried to cultivate the virus they were sure lay within the samples. But their efforts proved fruitless. Unable to return for further samples at that time, Hultin was forced to give up his search. But he never completely forgot his desire to find the Spanish flu virus.

For forty years, during which time he had a successful career as a pathologist and raised a family in San Francisco, Hultin kept an eye out for any new discoveries about the Spanish flu. Finally, in March 1997, he saw what he had been waiting for.

The journal *Science* had published an article by Dr. Jeffrey Taubenberger. After two years of research, Taubenberger and his associates had deciphered a small part of the genetic code of the Spanish flu virus.

EIGHTY-YEAR-OLD LUNGS

Dr. Taubenberger was the chief of the Division of Molecular Pathology at the Armed Forces Institute of Pathology (AFIP) in Washington, D.C. In 1995 he and a technician, Ann Reid, had learned that the National Tissue Repository had seventy samples of lung tissue from soldiers who had died of the

Spanish flu virus. Although neither had worked on influenza projects before, they decided to dissect the lung samples to see if they could isolate and decode the genetic makeup of the 1918 virus. Doing so might help scientists and medical researchers understand why this particular flu virus had been so lethal.

The repository's lung samples were plentiful. But only one, that of Roscoe Vaughan, a twenty-one-year-old private who had died at Camp Jackson, South Carolina, provided Taubenberger and his team with the material they needed. For more than a year, they studied and manipulated the tiny, fragile sample. Finally, they isolated a portion of the virus's genetic code.

Taubenberger's discovery was remarkable, but his research was far from complete. In order to get the entire code, he would need more tissue samples. It was around this time that Hultin read the *Science* article and decided to contact Taubenberger.

Hultin explained his interest in the Spanish flu and his effort forty years earlier in Brevig. He wondered if Taubenberger might like him to go back to Brevig to try to find additional lung samples. If so, he was prepared to leave for Alaska almost immediately.

Taubenberger took Hultin up on his offer. He was excited but cautious. Hultin's venture might not yield results. What were the chances that after forty years the bodies were still in the right condition or that Hultin would even be allowed access to the graves?

Dr. Jeffrey Taubenberger examines data on the genetic material of the 1918 flu virus.

There was only one way to find out. Hultin left for Alaska in August 1997 to see what he could dig up.

THE SPITSBERGEN PROJECT

Kirsty Duncan exhumed the bodies of flu victims on the remote island of Spitsbergen, Norway.

Across the Atlantic, in the small port town of Longyearbyen on the Norwegian island of Spitsbergen, Kirsty Duncan was hard at work trying to obtain the same kind of lung samples Taubenberger was seeking. Duncan was a medical geographer and climatologist (a person who studies the medical effects of geography and climate on humans). In 1993 she had become interested in the Spanish flu.

Like Hultin, Duncan believed that frozen bodies held the key to unlocking the Spanish flu virus. Her research had led her to the graves of seven young miners, all flu victims, buried at Longyearbyen. If all went well, she and her team would be able to exhume and autopsy the bodies sometime in the winter of 1997–1998.

Duncan went public with her plans early on. She wanted everyone to know that she planned to take extreme caution when digging up and handling the bodies. She acknowledged the dangers the mission could bring, the worst being the chance that somehow the decades-old virus would infect someone.

"As a member of the public, I would not want to think that some scientist just went up there and did this work," she said. "I would want to know about it, I would want to know that they did it responsibly and that they did it right. I would want them to debate the merits and drawbacks of the work."

Hultin, on the other hand, was quiet about his mission in Alaska. Unlike the Spitsbergen project, which involved virologists, pathologists, and professional excavators and was followed step-by-step by the media, his expedition team was made up of himself and a few villagers willing to dig up eighty-year-old corpses. The only thing holding up his expedition was permission from tribal elders. On August 19, 1997, he received that permission. He began his excavation that very day.

On the fourth day of digging, he found what he was looking for. There, laid out before him in a seven-foot-deep grave, was a woman who had died nearly eighty years earlier. Hultin knew at a glance that her lungs would be well preserved. That was partly because of the permafrost, and also because the woman had been obese and her lungs were surrounded by layers of insulating fat.

"I sat on a pail—turned upside down—and looked at her," Hultin recalled. "I gave her a name, Lucy. Donald Johanson had sat in Ethiopia in 1974 and looked at a skeleton that shed light on human evolution. He had named her Lucy. I also thought of Lucy, *lux*, Latin for light. She would help Taubenberger shed light on that pandemic."

Hultin removed Lucy's frozen lungs, sliced them, and set them in a preservative for the trip home. Back in San Francisco, he separated the frozen lung samples into four parcels. He mailed the specimens to Taubenberger in four separate packages to ensure that at least one would arrive safely. Despite the fact that he had packed the samples so that they would remain frozen in transit, there was some danger involved in mailing them. Had one of the packages been damaged, there was the possibility, though very remote, that the virus could escape. Fortunately all four packages arrived intact.

Within a week of receiving the samples, Taubenberger and Ann Reid knew that Hultin's work had paid off. There was no doubt that the lungs contained the virus and the genetic material they needed.

Taubenberger knew he owed a debt to the citizens of Brevig. He also knew that the media might storm their tiny village once word of his findings got out. Therefore, he requested their permission to make his research public. Until he received that permission, he would say nothing.

For five months the villagers considered the question. During this time, Kirsty Duncan drew closer to the start of her Spitsbergen excavation. Like the rest of the world, she knew nothing of Lucy or Taubenberger's findings.

That changed on December 4, 1997. Taubenberger was part of a panel of scientists meeting to discuss the final planning stages of Duncan's project. The rest of the panel was made up of some of the world's most prestigious virologists and medical researchers. During the meeting, Duncan stated that the only known sample of the Spanish flu virus was the one Taubenberger had obtained from the lungs of Private Roscoe Vaughan at the National Tissue Repository.

Taubenberger wrestled with a question of ethics: he had promised the Brevig villagers not to talk about Lucy until they gave their permission, yet he felt it was wrong not to speak up when he knew the medical community was being misinformed. In the end he decided to tell the panel that he had additional samples of the virus—but he wouldn't reveal where the samples had come from.

His announcement stunned the meeting into silence.

Then, as if nothing had happened, they continued to discuss Duncan's plans.

Taubenberger was perplexed, but he didn't say anything more about the additional samples at that time. A month later, however, he once again stated to the medical community that he had several lung samples with the flu virus.

For Duncan, Taubenberger's announcement was a blow. Lucy had revealed to Taubenberger what Duncan hoped her seven Norwegian miners would reveal to her. Taubenberger had beaten her to the punch.

To make matters worse, when the Spitsbergen excavation finally took place in August 1998, the miners' bodies proved to be badly decomposed. They had been buried near the surface rather than deep in the permafrost. Despite this disappointment, the team took tissue samples that they hoped would yield some useful information. Their research on the samples is still ongoing.

Until the Spanish flu is fully understood, getting a flu shot annually is the best way to keep the disease at bay.

THE SEARCH CONTINUES

Taubenberger and his team also continue to work on solving the mystery of the Spanish flu. It may take years for them to unravel the virus's entire genetic code. They already have a small portion of it, but their lung samples still may prove to be insufficient to yield a complete answer. In addition, in order to understand how the 1918 virus differed from earlier, less deadly flu viruses, they would need flu virus samples from earlier flu outbreaks. Finding such samples may not be possible.

The efforts of Dr. Jeffrey Taubenberger, Kirsty Duncan, and Dr. Johan Hultin have helped track down a killer. Their research has brought the flu's deadly past back into the public eye. Still, as Taubenberger puts it, while "we definitely have the right suspect . . . we do not yet know how the murder was committed."

Too many pieces of the puzzle are still missing, too many questions remain unanswered. What was the virus like before it mutated into its lethal form, and how and why did it mutate? Why did it break out of its usual pattern of killing only the old, the very young, and the weak? Does it still exist somewhere in the world, and if so, where? Could birds or mammals be acting as a repository for the deadly disease? And perhaps most important of all, will medical science be able to stop such a virus from killing again?

❦

ARMED AND READY

❦

THE 1918 INFLUENZA PANDEMIC left an indelible stamp on the world. It circled the globe in little more than a year, sickening and killing millions. It brought economies to a standstill, left families torn apart, and baffled doctors.

Today the medical community is much better prepared to stop the flu should it unleash such a lethal attack on the world again. The Centers for Disease Control (CDC) in Atlanta, Georgia, maintains a careful watch each flu season, ready to implement a plan of attack should influenza seem about to become epidemic or deadly. The World Health Organization (WHO) also monitors influenza. WHO receives information

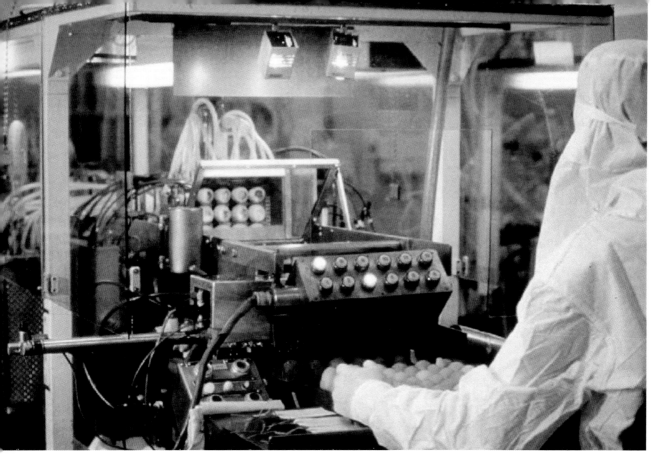

Each year, pharmaceutical companies produce millions of doses of flu vaccine.

about outbreaks from a 120-station global surveillance network. Like the CDC, it has a plan in place to control epidemics before they get out of hand.

In November and December 1997 both organizations were forced to implement their plans. Eighteen people in Hong Kong had sickened with a new kind of flu. Six people died from it. The numbers were small, but the proportion of people dying to those surviving—one out of every three—was terrifying.

Investigators and scientists from WHO, the CDC, and other international medical agencies made thorough inquiries into the situation. They worked quickly to isolate the origin of the flu—chickens sold at market in Hong Kong. Apparently the disease had spread from the chickens to their human handlers. Scientists called it the avian flu (from the Latin word *avis*, meaning "bird"). They worked quickly to create a vaccine and immunize people who had likely come into contact

THE 1918 INFLUENZA PANDEMIC

with the deadly virus. Their efforts led to the necessary destruction of nearly 1.5 million chickens—and the end of the outbreak.

Hong Kong was the site of a more puzzling case in 1999, when two children fell ill with flu symptoms. The virus they had contracted was identified as Type A (H9N2), a strain that usually infects only birds. The children recovered and no new cases were found, but scientists continue to be mystified as to how the children became infected in the first place.

In the years since these scares, medical researchers have developed new antiviral drugs that lessen the severity and duration of the flu. These new drugs seem to keep the growth of the virus in check. And thanks to Dr. Taubenberger and other researchers, we have enough knowledge about the 1918 flu virus that a vaccine could be formulated to protect people from it should it resurface.

For most people, the flu remains a disease of inconvenience, something to be avoided if possible but tolerated if contracted. We may be lucky enough to never again experience the deadly dance of the Spanish Lady. But if we do, we stand as armed and ready as we can be.

Meanwhile, new and unknown viruses have croppped up unexpectedly. On November 16, 2002, in China's Foshan City, one such virus began a seven-month attack that eventually sickened more than 8,400 people in over thirty countries and killed close to 800. The disease, dubbed Severe Acute Respiratory Syndrome, or SARS, has symptoms similar to pneumonia—high fever, headache, and body aches followed by increasing difficulty in breathing. However, this sickness didn't respond to the usual treatments given pneumonia patients. While some patients recovered from SARS, one out of every ten died when their lungs could no longer function.

Health officials worldwide responded quickly to the new threat. Travelers were warned to steer clear of SARS hotspots such as Shanghai, China, and Toronto, Canada, in an effort to stop the disease from spreading further. Individuals who did travel to these and other hard-hit places were told to remain at home for ten days after their return and to report to a hospital immediately if they showed any symptoms. In an eerie replay of the 1918 flu epidemic, many people started wearing surgical masks to keep SARS from entering their bodies.

All these efforts seemed to pay off. By early June 2003, the number of SARS cases had dwindled. Yet scientists continue to struggle with the disease. While the virus that causes SARS has been identified, there is no cure or vaccine for the disorder at this time. Until there is, a very real chance remains that SARS, like the flu, could re-emerge to add more victims to its list of casualties.

TIME LINE OF THE 1918 PANDEMIC

1918

March: Private Albert Gitchell comes down with Spanish influenza at Fort Riley, Kansas. First wave begins.

April: Six members of the Fifteenth Cavalry die of flu complications while sailing to France.

May: U.S. soldiers from Fort Riley bring influenza to France. Great Britain's Royal Navy is stricken. Flu reaches North Africa.

June: The first wave of influenza hits India, Japan, China, and the Philippines. Cuba, Puerto Rico, the Panama Canal Zone, and Hawaii are also stricken.

July: Height of the epidemic. Switzerland, Denmark, Norway, and Russia succumb.

August: First wave dies down at the beginning of the month. Second wave begins in Brest, France; Freetown, Sierra Leone; and Boston, Massachusetts at the end of the month. New Zealand is also hit.

September: Second wave strikes at military camps throughout the United States and begins to infect American civilians. Boston is the first major city to be hard hit.

October: Philadelphia, San Francisco, and other U.S. cities suffer major outbreaks. Remote corners of the world report flu outbreaks and deaths.

November: Second wave comes to an end in the United States early in the month but continues to strike elsewhere in the world until late in the month. World War I ends on November 11.

December: Third wave begins.

1919

January: Third wave reaches its height in the United States.

April: President Woodrow Wilson nearly dies of the disease.

May: Third wave dies out.

1951

Johan Hultin digs up the body of a little girl who died of Spanish flu; lung samples prove worthless.

1997

Jeffrey Taubenberger publishes an article in *Science* magazine, reporting work on lung samples from the National Tissue Repository. Hultin digs up "Lucy," providing Taubenberger with additional lung samples.

1998

Kirsty Duncan digs up the badly decomposed bodies of seven miners on Spitsbergen Island, Norway.

OTHER INFLUENZA PANDEMICS, EPIDEMICS, AND SCARES

1781

Influenza pandemic; influenza is given its name.

1847–48

First well-recorded pandemic.

1889

"Chinese distemper" influenza pandemic.

1957–1958

Asian flu kills 70,000 Americans, 98,000 people worldwide.

1968–1969

Hong Kong flu kills 34,000 Americans, 46,000 people worldwide.

1976

Swine flu scare; 40 million Americans are immunized; no outbreak occurs.

1997

Avian flu sickens eighteen people, kills six.

1999

Type A (H9N2) flu in Hong Kong sickens two children; both recover; investigations into disease continue.

November 16, 2002

First case of SARS identified.

June 17, 2003

WHO lifts travel advisories for all SARS hotspots except Beijing, China.

GLOSSARY

antibodies substances produced by the body to attack and defend against viruses or bacteria

armistice an agreement to stop fighting; a truce

attrition the gradual wearing away or weakening through constant stress

bacillus any type of rod-shaped bacteria

bacterium a single-celled microscopic organism; some kinds of bacteria cause disease in humans

cyanosis a health condition in which the skin turns blue from lack of oxygenated blood

disembarkation the act of leaving a ship

epidemic an outbreak of a deadly disease that affects a large number of people in a particular region

immunity the ability of the body to resist attacks by viruses and bacteria

mutated changed, altered

pandemic an outbreak of a deadly disease that affects a large portion of the world at about the same time

pathologist a person who studies the nature of disease

quarantine the keeping of a person, animal, or thing (such as a ship) away from others to stop the spread of a disease; to put someone or something in quarantine

vaccine live or dead virus, bacteria, or other chemicals that are injected into the body to produce immunity

virologist; virology a person who studies viruses; the study of viruses

virus a submicroscopic agent made up of genetic material surrounded by a shell of proteins, which invades a host in order to reproduce

TO FIND OUT MORE

BOOKS

Aronson, Virginia. *The Influenza Pandemic of 1918*. Philadelphia: Chelsea House, 2000.

A good overview of the pandemic, written for young adults.

Altman, Linda Jacobs. *Plague and Pestilence: A History of Infectious Disease*. Springfield, NJ: Enslow Books, 1998.

A well-written overview of a variety of diseases, including a section on influenza.

Getz, David. *Purple Death: The Mysterious Flu of 1918*. New York: Henry Holt, 2000.

Written for young adults, an overview of the 1918 influenza pandemic and a look at the current research into the virus.

Hoff, Brent, and Carter Smith III. *Mapping Epidemics: A Historical Atlas of Disease*. New York: Franklin Watts, 2000.

An interesting book with maps and text that describe the spread of many infectious diseases, including influenza.

ON THE INTERNET*

"The American Experience: Influenza 1918" at

http://www.pbs.org/wgbh/amex/influenza

A wonderful site that includes first-person accounts of the flu in the United States. Based on the television show produced for PBS.

"Doughboy's Lungs Yield 1918 Flu Virus" at

http://www.sciencenews.org

An interesting article detailing Dr. Jeffrey Taubenberger's discovery of Private Roscoe Vaughan's lung samples.

*All Internet sites were available and accurate when this book was sent to press.

"Influenza" at

> http://www.cdc.gov/ncidod/diseases/flu/viruses.htm
> The official influenza site of the Centers for Disease Control.
> Includes links to the CDC's current plan to combat outbreaks of
> influenza, statistics on vaccines, and information on past outbreaks.

"Influenza" at

> http://www.who.int/inf-fs/en/fact211.html
> A fact sheet on influenza by the World Health Organization.
> Includes information about WHO's surveillance network.

"The 1918 Influenza Pandemic" at

> http://www.stanford.edu/group/virus/uda/
> Although difficult to read because of the background color, a
> very informative site about the pandemic.

"1918 Spanish Flu Pandemic" at

> http://www.ninthday.com/spanish_flu.htm
> An overview of the pandemic, plus links to an interview with
> Dr. Jeffrey Taubenberger.

VIDEO

The American Experience: Influenza 1918.
> A fine hour-long video produced for public television in 1989.

BIBLIOGRAPHY

Aronson, Virginia. *The Influenza Pandemic of 1918.* Philadelphia:
Chelsea House, 2000.

Bray, R. S. *Armies of Pestilence: The Impact of Disease on History.*
New York: Barnes and Noble Books, 1996.

Collier, Richard. *The Plague of the Spanish Lady: The Influenza
Pandemic of 1918–1919.* Forge Village, MA: Murray Printing
Company, 1974.

Crosby, Alfred W., Jr. *America's Forgotten Pandemic*. Cambridge,
MA: Cambridge University Press, 1989.

————. *Epidemic and Peace 1918*. Westport, CT: Greenwood Press,
1976.

Davies, Pete. *The Devil's Flu: The World's Deadliest Influenza
Epidemic and the Scientific Hunt for the Virus that Caused It*.
New York: Henry Holt, 2000.

Getz, David. *Purple Death: The Mysterious Flu of 1918*. New York:
Henry Holt, 2000.

Hoehling, A. A. *The Great Epidemic: When the Spanish Influenza
Struck*. Boston: Little, Brown and Company, 1961.

Hoff, Brent, and Carter Smith III. *Mapping Epidemics: A Historical
Atlas of Disease*. New York: Franklin Watts, 2000.

Kolata, Gina. *Flu: The Story of the Great Influenza Pandemic of
1918 and the Search for the Virus that Caused It*. New York:
Farrar, Straus, Giroux, 1999.

NOTES ON QUOTATIONS

The quotations in this book are from the following sources:

Chapter One: What Is Influenza?

p. 1: "Until proof to the contrary," Hoehling, *The Great
Epidemic*, p. 3.

p. 6: "This disease," Aronson, *The Influenza Pandemic of 1918*, p. 37.

p. 7: "A Strange Form of Disease," Davies, *The Devil's Flu*, p. 59.

Chapter Two: The First Wave

p. 9: "The number of sick," Aronson, *The Influenza Pandemic of
1918*, p. 49.

p. 15: "In the midst," Hoehling, *The Great Epidemic*, p. 18.

p. 16: "It was a grievous business," Kolata, *Flu*, p. 11.

Chapter Three: The Second Wave

p. 19: "I had a little bird," Hoehling, *The Great Epidemic*, p. 33.

p. 22: "The congestion of the ship," Aronson, *The Influenza Pandemic of 1918*, p. 58.

p. 22: "unless precautions," Crosby, *Epidemic and Peace 1918*, p. 40.

p. 22: "spread rapidly," ibid.

p. 24: "[There are] hundreds of," Kolata, *Flu*, p. 16.

p. 24: "[The soldiers] rapidly develop," ibid., p. 14.

p. 25: "It takes Special trains," ibid.

p. 26: "This must be," ibid., p. 17.

p. 26: "It shocked me," Crosby, *Epidemic and Peace 1918*, p. 9.

p. 30: "As their lungs filled," "1918 Spanish Flu Pandemic" at http://www.ninthday.com/spanish_flu.htm

p. 31: "Telephone Service Faces a Crisis," "The Flu of 1918" at http://www.upenn.edu/gazette/1198/lynch2.html

p. 34: "Obey the laws," Hoehling, *The Great Epidemic*, p. 161.

p. 35: "Women of San Francisco," Crosby, *Epidemic and Peace 1918*, p. 97.

Chapter Four: The End of the War and the Flu

p. 39: "It has attacked the troops," Hoehling, *The Great Epidemic*, p. 152.

p. 44: "I am not going," Kolata, *Flu*, p. 49.

p. 46: "It would be quite easy," Crosby, *Epidemic and Peace 1918*, p. 47.

p. 47: "the skin is," Aronson, *The Influenza Pandemic of 1918*, p.77.

Chapter Five: The Search for the Killer

p. 49: "Working on the 1918 virus," Aronson, *The Influenza Pandemic of 1918*, p. 24.

p. 52: "As a member of the public," Kolata, *Flu*, p. 251.

p. 53: "I sat on a pail," ibid., pp. 262–263.

p. 56: "we definitely have," ibid., p. 305.

INDEX

ABOUT THE AUTHOR

STEPHANIE TRUE PETERS grew up in Westborough, Massachusetts. After graduating with a degree in history from Bates College, she moved to Boston, where she worked as an editor of children's books. She made the jump from editor to writer soon after the birth of her son. Since then, she has authored a number of nonfiction books for young people, including the other titles in the *Epidemic!* series. Stephanie lives in Mansfield, Massachusetts, with her husband, Dan, and their two children, Jackson and Chloe. She enjoys going on adventures with her family, beachcombing on Cape Cod, and teaching kick–boxing classes at the local YMCA.